A brief gu Sherbo Shaftesbury and Blandford

words and photographs by
Robert Westwood
© 2011 Robert Westwood
Contains Ordnance Survey data © Crown copyright and database right (2011)

ISBN 978-0-9564104-3-6

Inspiring Places Publishing
2 Down Lodge Close
Alderholt
Fordingbridge
Hampshire
SP6 3JA

JURASSICCOAST
QUALITY
BUSINESS

Contents:

Page

Introduction

Blandford, Sherborne and Shaftesbury are three old towns in north Dorset steeped in history. Surrounded by verdant countryside and charming villages, they have lots to interest those willing to travel and explore at a gentle pace. Their attractions are for those who appreciate history, culture and tranquil rural beauty.

This guide will lead you around this beautiful region, describing and explaining features of the landscape, important historical events, the growth of the three towns and suggesting things to do and places to visit. There are also several walks to do which can be enjoyed by all the family. Finally, with many superb illustrations, it will provide a lasting souvenir of this wonderful part of Dorset.

The map below shows the area covered by the book. It basically comprises a triangle formed by the main roads connecting the three towns although mention is made of one or two interesting places slightly outside this triangle.

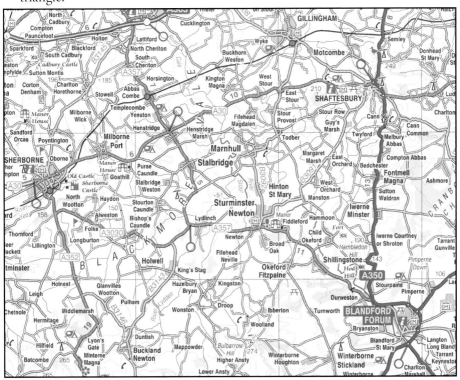

The Landscape

Hambledon Hill with the village of Child Okeford and the Blackmore Vale beyond.

The landscape of this part of northern Dorset reflects its geology. The Chalk forms a broad backbone to the county, running roughly north-east to south-west. Either side of it are lowlands formed from softer sands and clays; younger Tertiary sediments to the south, but older, Jurassic deposits to the north. We approach Shaftesbury from the south-east on the Chalk ridge, enjoying stunning vistas over the Vale of Blackmore. The various roads have to descend the escarpment, the B3081 from Cranborne doing so via the aptly named Zig-Zag Hill. We must climb up again to reach Shaftesbury, for the town is on an outcrop of another relatively hard rock, the Greensand, formed in the Cretaceous period just before the Chalk.

As we travel westwards from Shaftesbury towards Sherborne we cross the broad Vale of Blackmore, rich farmland on the clays and sands of the Jurassic. This picture continues as we travel south-eastwards from Sherborne to Blandford but as we near the town we join the valley of the beautiful River Stour at Sturminster Newton and see the high land of the Chalk again to our left with the magnificent hillfort of Hambledon Hill carved into its westernmost outlier.

When we explore Sherborne and its surrounding villages we might note that there are many fine buildings of golden limestone, similar to that found in the Cotswolds. The sediments of the Blackmore Vale are not all sands and clays. At times in the Upper Jurassic conditions were right for the formation of oolitic limestone. This hard stone forms as dissolved calcium carbonate precipitates around tiny sand or shell fragments in a shallow, tropical sea and is rolled backwards and forwards by the action of the waves. The tiny, spherical ooids (from the Greek for egg) can just about be seen with the naked eye. Portland Stone is a similar but younger limestone, the golden colour of the older rock is the result of the presence of iron.

Perhaps the best description of the contrasting landscapes of the Chalk uplands and the Vale of Blackmore comes from Thomas Hardy in *Tess of the D'Urbervilles*. He describes the change in scenery to someone who has travelled across the Chalk downs arriving at an escarpment with the vale stretching out below:

The traveller from the coast, who, after plodding northward for a score of miles over calcareous downs and corn-lands, suddenly reaches the verge of one of these escarpments, is surprised and delighted to behold, extended like a map beneath him, a country differing absolutely from that which he has passed through. Behind him the hills are open, the sun blazes down upon fields so large as to give an unenclosed character to the landscape, the lanes are white, the hedges low and plashed, the atmosphere colourless. Here, in the valley, the world seems to be constructed upon a smaller and more delicate scale; the fields are mere paddocks, so reduced that from this height their hedgerows appear a network of dark green threads overspreading the paler green of the grass. The atmosphere beneath is languorous, and is so tinged with azure that what artists call the middle distance partakes also of that hue, while the horizon beyond is of the deepest ultramarine. Arable lands are few and limited; with but slight exceptions the prospect is a broad rich mass of grass and trees, mantling minor hills and dales within the major. Such is the Vale of Blackmoor.

The Vale of Blackmore

Historical Notes

There is a great deal of historical interest in this area. Probably the earliest feature of note is the Neolithic "causewayed camp" on the south-east corner of Hambledon Hill. Archaeologists still debate whether these camps were fortified or served a more ceremonial function. The neighbouring Iron Age hillfort is one of many in Dorset; there is one right next door, just to the south, on Hod Hill. The Romans took these fortifications one by one in AD 43 as they completed the conquest of much of Britain. There was bitter fighting at some but it is likely that at others there was less of a struggle. At Hod Hill archaeologists found a collection of Roman "ballista" bolts at what appeared to be the largest Iron Age hut, suggesting the Romans had targeted the chieftain and that the community had then swiftly capitulated.

A long period of peaceful prosperity followed the Roman conquest. A fort was established on Hod Hill and Roman villas have been found at Iwerne Minster and Hinton St. Mary. Little is known about Dorset in the "Arthurian years" of the Dark Ages after the Romans left. Although the Saxons won a great victory over the Britons at Old Sarum in AD 552, Dorset was not occupied for some time, all we know is that by AD 700 the Saxons were in control of Dorset, maybe following a gradual process of integration and assimilation. The county became part of the great kingdom of Wessex and Shaftesbury and Sherborne were important towns. Shaftesbury was established as a defensive "burgh" by Alfred the Great

8

Little now remains of Shaftesbury Abbey but its pretty gardens and museum make it worth a visit. The statue represents its founder, King Alfred.

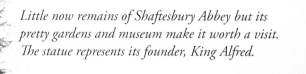

around AD 880. A number of these defensive settlements were constructed to protect the people against Viking raiders. Sherborne was at one stage the capital of Wessex and in AD 705 Aldhelm was appointed its first bishop.

In the 12th century Roger de Caen, Bishop of Salisbury and the second most powerful man in England, built a palace at Sherborne. He was arrested by King Stephen during the civil war with Matilda and the palace or castle was confiscated. Sherborne Castle also featured prominently in the English Civil War when it was besieged by the forces of Parliament (see page 13).

In the latter part of the Middle Ages the region prospered as a rich agricultural area. The fertile soils of the Vale of Blackmore were complimented by the Chalk downlands which were ideal for rearing sheep. Much of the land was under the control of the Church, but things changed following the dissolution of the monasteries in the 16th century and rich merchants and politicians became the new landlords. Sherborne Abbey escaped destruction and became a church, but the abbey at Shaftesbury was not so lucky.

In the 1720s Daniel Defoe published a series of accounts of his journeys through Britain. They provide a fascinating insight into life before the Industrial Revolution. Between Sherborne and Shaftesbury it was the vast flocks of sheep that made the biggest impression on him. There were literally hundreds of thousands of sheep on the downlands and Defoe says the shepherds were "everywhere in the way, and who, with a very little pains, a traveller may always speak with".

Dorset remained largely rural during and following the Industrial Revolution and during the 18th and 19th centuries conditions became steadily worse for the population dependent on farm labouring. In the "Captain Swing" riots of 1830 disaffected labourers smashed farm machinery around the county. Several violent incidents took place near Shaftesbury. It is easy to imagine that this region has always been one of peaceful, rural tranquility but back in the 19th century it was a dangerous place. Clashes between gamekeepers and poachers, smugglers and Revenue men were all too frequent!

Sandford Orcas Manor, north of Sherborne.

Shaftesbury

As mentioned previously, Shaftesbury was conceived in AD 880 by Alfred the Great, who recognised the defensive potential of a site over 700 feet above sea level and surrounded on three sides by steep slopes. A number of defensive "burghs" were created around Dorset in key positions. In AD 888 Alfred founded an abbey here and made his daughter the first abbess. Shaftesbury prospered and another great Saxon king, Athelstan, authorised the formation of two mints here to strike coins. In AD 979 the body of the murdered King Edward (later known as "the Martyr") was brought to the abbey from Wareham. When he was canonised in 1001 Shaftesbury's prosperity was guaranteed as it became a place of pilgrimage. The town was reputedly popular with King Canute who died here in 1035.

The abbey continued to prosper throughout the Middle Ages, enriched by the patronage of several kings. It was "dissolved" on the orders of Henry VIII in 1539 and most of the stone used for local building projects. Today only the foundations remain. Throughout most of its history Shaftesbury has been a small, prosperous market town and remains so today.

Thomas Hardy used Shaftesbury in his novels, calling it "Shaston". It features prominently in *Jude the Obscure* where Hardy describes it as follows:

"The natural picturesqueness and singularity of the town still remain; but strange to say these qualities, which were noted by many writers in ages when scenic beauty is said to have been unappreciated, are passed over in this, and one of the queerest and quaintest spots in England stands virtually unvisited to-day."

Gold Hill, Shaftesbury

In his book *Dorsetshire Folk-lore,* published in 1922, J. S. Udal recounts an annual custom of the town that was performed up to around 1830. Owing to its lofty position the town always had a problem with the supply of water. For centuries the people of Shaftesbury had to fetch water from wells in the neighbouring parish of Motcombe, until a deep artesian well was dug in the town in the early 19th century. Known as the "Bezant" ceremony, the inhabitants carried the bezant, some sort of ornate mace decorated with jewels and flowers, together with a calf's head and money, to the lord of the manor of Motcombe as thanks for the water.

Things to do:
- Walk down Gold Hill, made famous by the Hovis advert in the 1970s.
- Have something to eat or drink in one of the town's pubs, cafés or restaurants.
- Visit the abbey and admire the views across the Vale of Blackmore from the terrace outside the abbey.
- Visit the Gold Hill Museum and see its collections relating to the town's history.

Sherborne

Sherborne is one of Dorset's loveliest towns. Built with the local, golden Jurassic limestone and surrounded by beautiful countryside, it is a delight to wander around and soak up the atmosphere. It takes its name from the Old English "scire-burne", meaning "clear stream", a description of the River Yeo which flows through the town. There are a number of interesting places to visit; Sherborne has two castles, a magnificent abbey and a museum. As noted before, in 1722 Daniel Defoe set out on a journey around the whole of Britain and published his diaries of the travels in *A Tour Through the Whole Island of Great Britain*. Although not the county town, Defoe noted that Sherborne or "Shireburn", as it was in those days, was the most populous town in Dorset. He described the abbey as a "reverend pile"!

Sherborne came to prominence in AD 705 when King Ine of Wessex appointed Aldhelm as its first bishop. A Benedictine monastery was established there in 998 which continued until the Dissolution in 1539.

The town's importance grew in the early 12th century when a castle was built for Roger de Caen, Bishop of Salisbury. He was Chancellor to Henry I and at one time the second most powerful man in England. Following the King's death and the subsequent civil war between King Stephen and Matilda, Roger found himself on the wrong side and the castle was seized by the King.

Sherborne has remained a thriving market town for much of its history. It is still a thriving community and there is plenty to interest

visitors of all ages.

Things to do:
- Visit the abbey.
- Visit the old castle.
- Visit the new castle and/or walk round its lovely gardens.
- Explore the historic town centre and visit the museum.
- Have something to eat or drink in one of the town's many pubs,

Old Sherborne Castle

The old castle was built for Roger de Caen, Bishop of Salisbury in the early 12th century. It was a fortified palace and was built on a grand scale. After it was confiscated by King Stephen it remained in royal hands until it was returned to the Church for a while by Edward III. The great Elizabethan adventurer Sir Walter Raleigh fell in love with the castle and persuaded Elizabeth I to grant him the lease. He found it uninhabitable however, and had a new palace built in the grounds.

In the English Civil War, the castle was the scene of a fierce siege in 1645. It held out for many days in Royalist hands until the Parliamentarians under General Fairfax finally took it. It was subsequently slighted to prevent it being used again.

Opposite page: Sherborne Abbey. Below: Old Sherborne Castle.

"New" Sherborne Castle

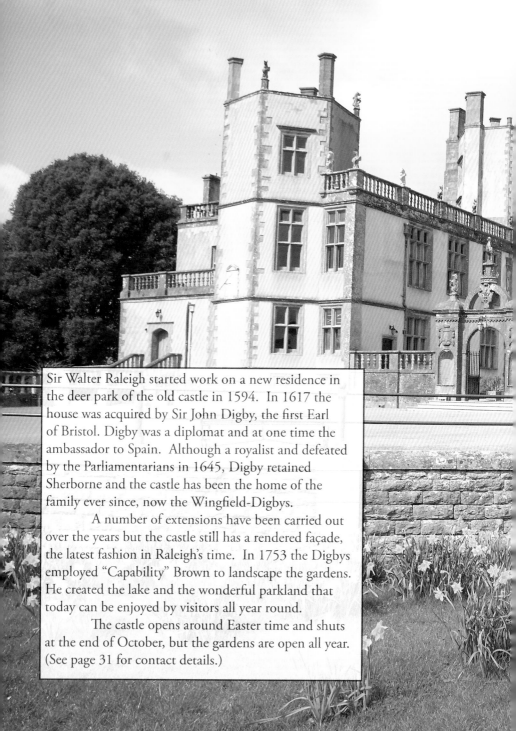

Sir Walter Raleigh started work on a new residence in the deer park of the old castle in 1594. In 1617 the house was acquired by Sir John Digby, the first Earl of Bristol. Digby was a diplomat and at one time the ambassador to Spain. Although a royalist and defeated by the Parliamentarians in 1645, Digby retained Sherborne and the castle has been the home of the family ever since, now the Wingfield-Digbys.

A number of extensions have been carried out over the years but the castle still has a rendered façade, the latest fashion in Raleigh's time. In 1753 the Digbys employed "Capability" Brown to landscape the gardens. He created the lake and the wonderful parkland that today can be enjoyed by visitors all year round.

The castle opens around Easter time and shuts at the end of October, but the gardens are open all year. (See page 31 for contact details.)

Raleigh's original building was rectangular and four storeys high. He later added hexagonal turrets to the four corners. Sir John Digby added four wings to Raleigh's design, giving the building its present shape.

Blandford Forum

For centuries Blandford Forum has been a prosperous market town serving the fertile Vale of Blackmore. It is still thriving today, aided by modern industrial growth and a successful brewery. It grew around a crossing point of the River Stour and was conveniently placed on main routes between Dorchester and Salisbury, and Poole and Shaftesbury.

In the early 19th century the town was devastated by two fires; the second leaving it almost totally destroyed. Two eminent local architects, the brothers John and William Bastard were responsible for the rebuilding programme. As a consequence Blandford is now one of the best examples in England of a Georgian town.

The Hall and Woodhouse brewery has been an important part of the economic life of Blandford since the 18th century and remains a major employer. It is still a family run business and there is a fascinating visitor centre. Tours of the brewery can also be arranged.

Blandford is also home to Bryanston, one of the region's leading public schools, and to the Royal Corps of Signals. Their camp lies just outside the town on the Salisbury road and has a lively and informative museum that is open all year.

In September the countryside near Blandford hosts the Great Dorset Steam Fair which attracts thousands of visitors from all over the world.

The River Stour at Blandford Forum.

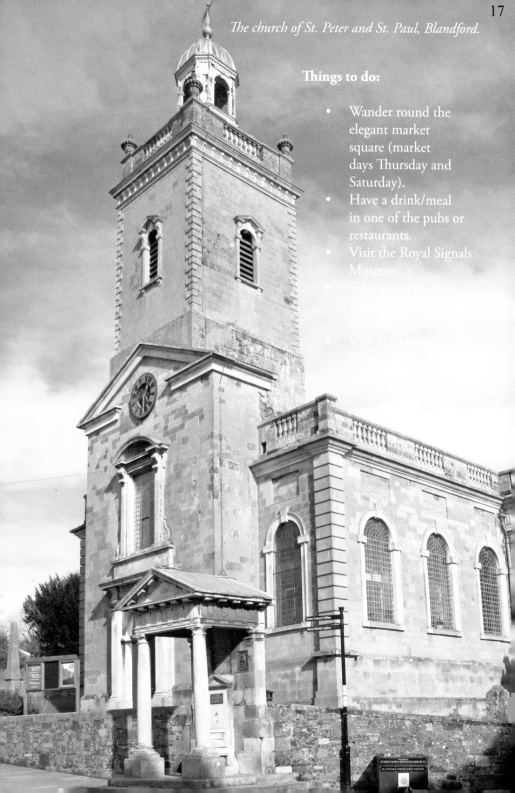

The church of St. Peter and St. Paul, Blandford.

Things to do:

- Wander round the elegant market square (market days Thursday and Saturday).
- Have a drink/meal in one of the pubs or restaurants.
- Visit the Royal Signals Museum.
- Take a tour of the Hall and Woodhouse brewery.
- Visit the Cavalcade of Costume.

Sturminster Newton

Sturminster Newton has always been the main market town for the Vale of Blackmore. It remains a lively, bustling place, especially on market days! The town centre is pretty and there are a great variety of buildings. It has two associations with eminent literary figures; William Barnes the Dorset poet was born near the town in 1801 and went to school here. A lot of his poetry describes the rural life of the area in the 19th century. Thomas Hardy moved to Sturminster Newton between 1876 and 1878, just after his marriage to Emma Gifford. He described his stay as idyllic and wrote *The Return of the Native* while at Riverside Villa.

On the River Stour which flows along the western and southern sides of the town are two places worth visiting. About 250 metres upstream from the town bridge is Sturminster Newton Mill. There has probably been a mill here since Saxon times and the present one dates from the 17th century. The mill is open during the summer. A little way downstream from the bridge is Fiddleford Manor (signposted from main road), part of a small stone manor house from the 14th century. It is maintained by English

Below: The River Stour near Fiddleford Mill. (See walk page 26.)

Top left: Fiddleford Manor, a 14th century manor house. Below right: Its wonderful roof timbers. Below left: Sturminster Newton Mill. There is parking and a picnic place next to the mill and you can walk along the River Stour to Hinton St. Mary. You can also walk a short distance upstream to Riverside Villa, once the home of Thomas Hardy (see page 30). Above right: The town bridge over the River Stour.

Heritage and entrance is free. The manor is renowned for its roof timbers, probably the finest in Dorset. (See walk page 26.)

Sturminster Newton also has a small museum in the town. (See information at end of book.)

Things to do:
- Explore the old town.
- Visit the town museum.
- Visit Fiddleford Manor.
- Visit Sturminster Newton Mill.
- Have a walk along the river. (See page 26.)

The Villages

As might be expected, there are some lovely villages in this historic region and it would be difficult to mention them all in so short a space. Below are some that the author thinks are worth visiting for a variety of reasons. All are shown on the map on page 3.

Ashmore – Said to be Dorset's highest village, Ashmore is a delightful, unspoilt village with a pond that possibly dates from Roman times. Remarkably, given its height of 700 feet, the pond rarely dries out. It was lined with clay and is basically a large dew pond. It has been colonised by ducks and makes a very photogenic setting.

Iwerne Courtney or Shroton – This is another village with a beautiful setting, at the foot of Hambledon Hill. It is a good starting point for a walk on Hambledon and has a nice pub (The Cricketers) to finish in. Following the Clubmen's Rebellion in the English Civil War, when local men staged a last stand on Hambledon, prisoners were locked in the church overnight by Oliver Cromwell to teach them a lesson. (See page 25.)

Compton Abbas – A pretty village at the foot of the Chalk escarpment of Fontmell Down. Nearby, on top of the Chalk, is Compton Abbas Airfield, a quaint little grass airfield with a charming café where one can have lunch or tea inside, or on the terrace and watch the comings and goings of the light aircraft.

The pond at Ashmore.

Above: Compton Abbas Airfield. Below: The church at Purse Caundle.

Child Okeford -
Quite a large village
with a lovely centre
and two good pubs,
The Baker Arms and
The Saxon Inn. The
village is on the west
side of Hambledon
Hill and is another
good base from which
to explore the hill.

Purse Caundle – A
quiet backwater with a
pretty church, but its main attraction is a superb manor house that is open
on some afternoons each week during the summer. (See information page 31
or check with Sherborne TIC.)

Sandford Orcas – A little, picturesque place with another wonderful manor
house built from the local golden coloured Ham Stone. This too is open
some afternoons during the summer (see page 31) and a guided tour is given
by the owner.

Walk 1 - Ashmore, Dorset's highest village

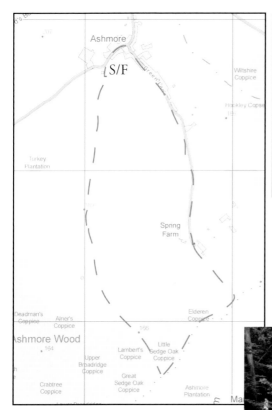

Distance: About 3 miles
Time: 1.5 hours
Starting Point:
GR 912178 (Explorer 118)
Notes:
An easy, fairly level walk.

Dogs: No problem, they might have to be on lead near the farm.

This is a very simple walk to follow amid beautiful and varied scenery. It is usually possible to park somewhere in the village of Ashmore. Walk past the church heading west and take a left turn down a bridleway known as Halfpenny Lane. This is in fact the Wessex Ridgeway. Follow this into Ashmore Wood [signed Great Peaky Coppice]. When the path reaches the end of the wood turn left to Tollard Green. Follow this path until you come to a small valley. At the bottom of this take the path on the left to Well Bottom. At Well Bottom the path becomes a small road, follow this back to Ashmore village.

Walk 2 - Hambledon Hill, Iron Age hillfort

There is a small car park at the foot of Hod Hill (GR ST853113). From here walk a little way to the right up the road. There is a cottage on the left; take the footpath to the right of the cottage leading up the hill. At the top of the hill take the path to the left. Follow this across what was a Neolithic Camp. Carry on past the trig. point, through a gate and follow the path around the ramparts of the hillfort on the right (eastern) side of the hill.

At the far end of the hill, as the path begins to descend, go left and climb up the ramparts. You are free to wander over the hillfort so choose your level and follow the ramparts back around the hill to the gate where you entered. The views on the western side of the hill are even more breathtaking. Go past the trig. point again and then turn right through a gate (marked footpath). Go straight across the field to the fence and turn left, keeping the fence on your right.

At the bottom of the field go through the gate and follow the path to the road, keeping the wood on your right. Turn left at the road and follow it back to the car park.

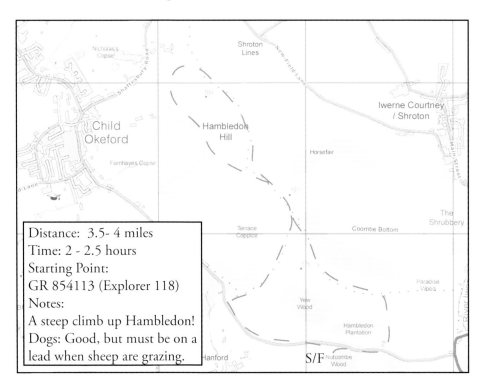

Distance: 3.5- 4 miles
Time: 2 - 2.5 hours
Starting Point:
GR 854113 (Explorer 118)
Notes:
A steep climb up Hambledon!
Dogs: Good, but must be on a lead when sheep are grazing.

24

Hambledon Hill at sunset.

This is one of my favourite parts of Dorset: quiet, peaceful, beautiful and with a fascinating history. In early summer both Hod and Hambledon Hills are ablaze with wild flowers and at any time of the year the views from the tops are worth the effort, particularly in early evening sunlight.

The walk itself does not take in Hod Hill, although the suggested car park is at its foot and it is a short, although fairly steep, climb up for those feeling energetic. This north-west corner is where the Roman fort was sited following the defeat of the Durotriges tribe whose settlement this was.

Once you have completed the initial climb the path takes you across a saddle of the hill where a Neolithic "causewayed camp" was situated. This ancient settlement or meeting place was initiated around 5-6000 years ago. Its name derives from the path leading to such sites and has led archaeologists to believe that they were probably not defensive structures. The remains of animal bones and pots has suggested to some that they were important ceremonial centres. A large cemetery was excavated at Hambledon where it was found that about 60% of the remains were of children.

The remains of the Iron Age hillfort are unmistakable; steep ramparts cut into the side of the hill. They were made simply by digging a ditch and throwing the earth in front to make a bank. It's not difficult to appreciate that a lot of work was involved! Hambledon must have been a major centre for the Durotriges tribe. Unfortunately it seems their fortifications, which are numerous in Dorset, were designed to defend against neighbouring settlements. They were clearly organised and capable people and who knows what they might have achieved had they planned co-operatively to fight the Roman invasion.

Hambledon was the scene of a curious episode during the English Civil War. Gangs of "Clubmen" had gathered in a number of counties; local men, typically farm labourers, who were fed up with the deprivations caused by the war. Armies of both sides requisitioned supplies from the countryside they moved through, often sending out parties of soldiers to simply take what they needed. The Dorset Clubmen aimed to protect their land and their families and warned both Royalist and Parliamentary forces that they would be challenged. It was a brave and perhaps desperate action; they had little military training, poor weapons and were no match for battle hardened professional troops. Oliver Cromwell was sent to take care of the Dorset Clubmen who had encamped on Hambledon Hill. They were quickly overcome with few casualties, most fled. As a warning some prisoners were locked in nearby Shroton church overnight and released after a lecture in the morning.

Walk 3 - Sturminster Newton, along the River Stour

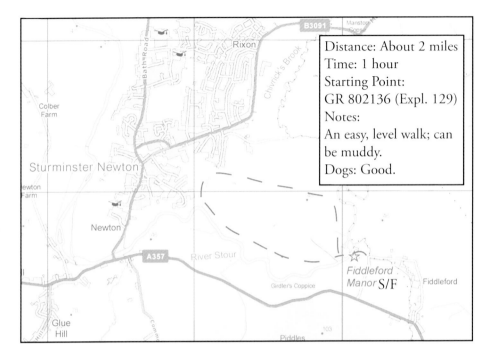

Distance: About 2 miles
Time: 1 hour
Starting Point:
GR 802136 (Expl. 129)
Notes:
An easy, level walk; can
be muddy.
Dogs: Good.

The walk begins in the car park of Fiddleford Manor, signposted off the A357 just east of Sturminster Newton. It is well worth having a look at the manor at the beginning or end of the walk. Walk down the small road past the car park and turn left towards Fiddleford Mill. Turn left when you come to the river and follow the path across a small footbridge to the other side of the River Stour. Now follow the river to the old railway line and turn left along it towards the town. When you come to a small bridge go down the path to the right and back under the bridge. Follow the footpath signs to the river and then follow the path back to Fiddleford Manor.

The River Stour

Walk 4 - Sherborne, around the castles

This walk starts by the railway level crossing at the end of South Street. There is a car park nearby off Ludbourne Road opposite Sainsburys. Cross over the B3145 (New Road) and you will see a footpath directly opposite over a stile. Take this path and turn left towards Sherborne Castle. Keep following the path; it will take you across open fields with great views of the castle and its parkland. You will come to a small lodge by a wooded area. Continue up the hill and bear right at the top, continuing to follow the path. You will go through an enclosed wooded area past some farm buildings. Turn left at the end on a small road and follow the path, turning right as you reach the drive of a small cottage and then left through a wooded area. The path now descends through a deer park. Keep straight on and cross the stream at the bottom. You will reach the tiny hamlet of Pinford; turn left and then right across a field. Go through the big gateway at the top and follow the path through the woods. Turn left out of the woods after a short way and follow the path across the fields, under the railway, to the A30. You can then follow this the short distance back into Sherborne, following the signs for the town centre. There is a footpath all the way. When you reach the A30 be sure, first, to have a look at the ancient chancel of Saint Cuthbert.

Sherborne Castle

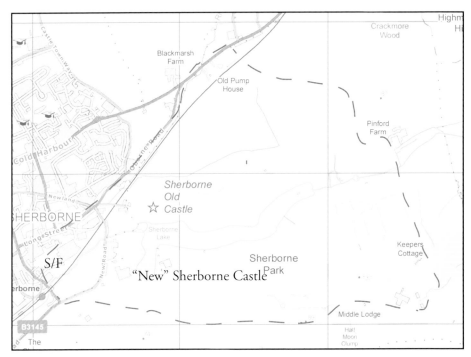

Distance: About 5 miles
Time: 2-2.5 hours
Starting Point:
GR 642162 (Explorer 129)
Notes: A lovely walk through varied countryside. Some great views of Sherborne Castle and its grounds. Take time to visit St. Cuthbert's Chancel.
Dogs: Good, but may need to be on a lead at times.

Right: Old St. Cuthbert's Chancel on the A30 at Oborne, just outside Sherborne. Only the chancel survives of a church built in the 16th century.

Walk 5 - Around Fontmell Down

Fontmell Down is a piece of Chalk grassland, bought by the National Trust in memory of Thomas Hardy. It commands stunning views over the Vale of Blackmore and is a haven for wild flowers and butterflies. It can be reached from Shaftesbury by following the B3081 south towards Melbury Abbas.

There are a number of walks that can be followed here but the one suggested is just a short stroll around the top of the down enabling you to savour the spectacular views. There is a small car park at the side of the road. From here simply walk out over Fontmell Down following the side of the hill. You will reach some Cross Dykes, linear earthworks of ancient origin. Go over these and turn left, through a gate and then turn left again back up the other side of the down and keeping at roughly the same

level. When you reach the road you will see there is a footpath by the side of it back to the car park.

If you wish you could walk to the pretty village of Compton Abbas and back on a circular route. See the OS Explorer 118 map.

Right: Fontmell Down

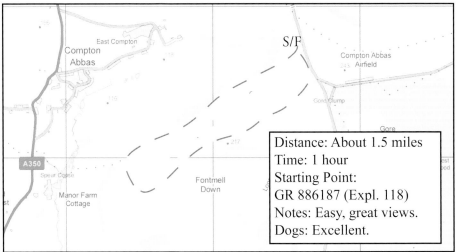

Distance: About 1.5 miles
Time: 1 hour
Starting Point:
GR 886187 (Expl. 118)
Notes: Easy, great views.
Dogs: Excellent.

Thomas Hardy Country

The rich farmland of the Vale of Blackmore provided the setting for one of Thomas Hardy's greatest and most famous novels, *Tess of the D'Urbervilles.* Hardy called it "The Vale of the Little Dairies". Tess was born and raised in the village of "Marlott", present day Marnhull. This is a large, sprawling village and the village pub, The Crown, was where Tess' father learned he was possibly related to the wealthy D'Urberville family, starting the whole

tragic story. The nearby church was where the vicar refused to let Tess bury her illegitimate baby.

Shaftesbury was called "Shaston" in Hardy's novels. It featured prominently in *Jude the Obscure* where Phillotson was the schoolmaster. It was also where Tess visited Angel Clare's family to seek their help. Sherborne, too, featured in one of Hardy's novels, *The Woodlanders.* Hardy called the town "Sherton Abbas".

As mentioned on page 18, Thomas Hardy lived for a while in Sturminster Newton, at Riverside Villa, just after his marriage to Emma Gifford. It was a very happy and productive period for him.

Top: The church at Marnhull.
Middle: The Crown public house at Marnhull, Tess' father's local.
Bottom: Riverside Villa at Sturminster Newton which Hardy rented for a while.

Useful Information

Sherborne, Shaftesbury and Blandford all have good tourist information centres which provide information about accommodation, attractions, travel and local events.
Sherborne TIC - 01935 815341
Shaftesbury TIC - 01747 853514
Blandford TIC - 01258 454770
Some useful websites:
www.shaftesburydorset.com - the town's official website.
www.shaftesburyheritage.org.uk - for information about the abbey and the Gold Hill Museum.
www.shaftesburyartscentre.org.uk - the Shaftesbury Arts Centre.
www.sherbornetown.com - has a list of local events.
www.gdsf.co.uk - the Great Dorset Steam Fair, held every September near Blandford.
www.statelyhomes.com - for information about the opening times of Sandford Orcas Manor.
www.britinfo.net - for information about Purse Caundle Manor.
www.sturminsternewton-museum.co.uk - for information about the opening of the mill and the town's museum.
www.sherbornecastle.com - the website of the "new" castle with full visitor information.
www.abbasair.com - the website for Compton Abbas Airfield - details of what's going on plus flying and flying lesson vouchers.
www.royalsignalsmuseum.com - for the Royal Signals Museum at Blandford.
www.sherbornemuseum.co.uk - for information about Sherborne's lovely little museum.
www.theblandfordfashionmuseum.com - Blandford's costume museum.

Other titles from *Inspiring Places Publishing:*

Ancient Dorset

Dark Age Dorset

Fossils and Rocks of the Jurassic Coast

The Jurassic Coast - Illustrated

The Life and Works of Thomas Hardy

Mysterious Places of Dorset

Smugglers' Dorset

Mystery Big Cats of Dorset

Historic Dorset

Day Tours in the East of Dorset

A brief guide to Purbeck

A brief guide to Weymouth, Portland and Dorchester

order online at www.inspiringplaces.co.uk

JURASSICCOAST
**QUALITY
BUSINESS**